I0463213

Online Marketing Success

Volume #1: The Best Of The Blog

Thom Lancaster
http://thomlancaster.com

Copyright © 2010 Thom Lancaster

All Rights Reserved. No part of this publication may be reproduced in any form or by any means, including scanning, photocopying, or otherwise without prior written permission of the copyright holder.

Disclaimer and Terms of Use: The Author and Publisher has strived to be as accurate and complete as possible in the creation of this book, notwithstanding the fact that he does not warrant or represent at any time that the contents within are accurate due to the rapidly changing nature of the Internet. While all attempts have been made to verify information provided in this publication, the Author and Publisher assumes no responsibility for errors, omissions, or contrary interpretation of the subject matter herein. Any perceived slights of specific persons, peoples, or organizations are unintentional. In practical advice books, like anything else in life, there are no guarantees of income made. Readers are cautioned to reply on their own judgment about their individual circumstances to act accordingly. This book is not intended for use as a source of legal, business, accounting or financial advice. All readers are advised to seek services of competent professionals in legal, business, accounting, and finance field.

With thanks to Dennis Becker from the Earn1KADay Insiders Club - and everyone who has supported me on my online journey.

Table of Contents

Introduction

Hello there, and the welcome to **Online Marketing Success – Volume #1: The Best Of The Blog**.

I'd like to take this opportunity to tell you a little about the thought-process behind this book, which is going to be the first in an occasional series (what that means is that I have no set release dates, or firm deadlines to work to).

Too often, excellent content ends up being posted onto a Web site somewhere, or constrained within an ebook, when really there's a big market for it offline. It's all about convenience. I have an Amazon Kindle, and I love it, but there's something about the feel of a published book that just makes everything seem real.

So, I've christened this series of books **Online Marketing Success**. Those of you who know me, will recognise this as the title of my Internet Marketing blog, which you can read and leave comments on by going to **http://thomlancaster.com**.

These are going to be short, snappy and to-the-point books. Not full of filler or anything that just isn't good content. I hope that's something, as a fellow online marketer, that you'll appreciate.

In this book, I've collected together for you a eight of my best posts from the blog, so that you can read them, reflect on them and be inspired by them wherever you may be. They cover a variety of internet marketing subjects, and they're intended so that you can just dip in and out of the book and read a section that interests you.

Wishing you every success with the tactics and ideas inside Volume #1 and here's to Volume #2!

Best wishes,

Thom Lancaster

Thom Lancaster

Four Steps To Success With Giveaway Events

If you're trying to build a list in the Internet Marketing niche, you've probably heard of Giveaway Events.

Essentially, how they work is as follows. You join the event as a contributor. You upload a 'gift' for people joining the event as Members. Then you collect their name and e-mail address to add to your autoresponder before they get to their download.

It's traditional 'bribe-based' list building, but on a large scale with a lot of other marketers participating.

But, how can you best make use of the list building opportunities afforded to you through Giveaway Events?

I've prepared four simple steps which you should follow to make sure you've getting every optin subscriber you can.

Step #1 – Prepare Gifts With A High Perceived Value

You need at least one gift, but if you have more than one it gives you more flexibility to test out different optin strategies and join multiple events.

The higher the perceived value of your gift, the more people who will opt in to your list in order to download it.

I've found that the following types of products work well:

- products that come with Private Label or other rights, so that the customers can resell them.

- video and audio products.

- product bundles (multiple e-books etc).

- software products.

The worst converting product for optins is generally the traditional e-book. Even if it's the best e-book in the world, people just don't tend to want to download it.

What do you do if you don't have a product? Find a product with resale rights, even if you have to pay a small amount of money for it, and offer that.

Chances are, if you're like me you've got a hard disk full of those sorts of materials already.

Step #2 – Set Up Your Optin List

You need an autoresponder, like Aweber, and a suitable squeeze page.

If you don't know what a squeeze page looks like, here's a squeeze page of mine.

Then set up a download page from which your product can be downloaded.

Make sure your autoresponder is set up so that when your optin subscriber confirms their e-mail address they get sent straight to the download page.

Step #3 – Choose a Giveaway Event

There are many Giveaway Events going on at any one time and you can choose any of these.

Generally, I've had the best results with the larger Giveaway Events. Essentially, these are ones that big marketers are behind. The reason for this is that there will be more traffic going to the Giveaway Event and you have the chance of more optins from it.

I'd also recommend that you get in well before the start of the Giveaway Event, to give your product maximum exposure.

Many Giveaway Events offer you the chance to pay for extra exposure. It is usually a good deal and should get you subscribers for a very low cost, but if you're just starting out you can skip this step.

Step #4 – Set Up Your Offer On The Giveaway Site

If you've followed Steps 1 to 3, this should be quite straightforward.

Most Giveaway Events use the same software, so this is a quick process once you know what you're doing.

First of all, you set up your profile, with your photo, Twitter account etc (this is excellent for personal branding).

Then you set up your gift, with the e-cover (if it doesn't come with an e-cover I suggest using a screenshot), location of the squeeze page and download page etc.

You also need to give a description of your product. You need catchy text here to get people to optin. State the benefits, and push the perceived value (e.g. if you're offering PLR make that really obvious).

Now, you just sit back and wait for your gifts to approve (normally a formality) and then the traffic to roll in. You'll need to tell your own list about the giveaway once it starts, as that's always a condition of participating, apart from that you're all set.

Optimising The Giveaway Process

The process is pretty simple, but there are a few things you can do to make it even more profitable for you.

Present a one-time offer to anyone who tries to join your list. That can get you an immediate income and get yourself a proven buyer, rather than simply a free loader.

You can always test out different offers, and, if you purchase the upsell at most Giveaways, you can put up multiple products. In this case, I'd recommend you make them as varied as possible to catch different sections of the market.

Super Successful Kids and Internet Marketing

I've come to a conclusion.

If the Internet had been around in its present form 15 years ago, I'd be a much more successful Internet Marketer than I am now!

Back then, the Internet was in its infancy, but I used to love computers and everything about them. I'd think nothing about sitting down for hours and writing a computer program, or composing material for a magazine distributed on floppy disk (yes, rather like a less convenient Internet).

I had few distractions.

And, I think that's the secret for many of the super successful kids who are doing well in the Internet Marketing field.

A lack of distractions.

Let's face it. Being younger, you don't have all of the same responsibilities that adults have. There are people there to look after you. No job, no mortgage, no people depending on you.

Even with increasing pressures on young people, both at school and outside, they have the one important commodity. Time, to develop into success.

So, kids go and develop your marketing skills while you can, as time to learn is something that's almost impossible to get back as you get older.

But, it's not all doom and gloom.

There's one thing that you develop as you get older. That's life experience. And, it tells you to work smarter.

How can you work smarter? By managing your time, and getting things done quicker and more effectively.

Use every spare moment. Develop systems to streamline different processes.

And that is how I think older marketers can be super successful, just like the kids!

Can Webinars Every Really Replace Products?

Over the past few days, I've been learning the secret of fast article writing and been ultra-productive with it. I can now turn around a quality article in 12 minutes and submit it to EzineArticles within that time (and don't underestimate the time it takes to fill in all the extra fields and information on EzineArticles).

That, in itself, is going to be an interesting tutorial for another time – but this also formed the basis for a number of email messages I sent out to my list.

At the end of it all, I asked my list how they would rather I presented the tutorial to them, and a number of people graciously responded.

Would they prefer me to record everything in a product?

Or, would they like me to hold a live webinar, show them the results, and take questions?

The results are in, and they might surprise you...

Here are the percentages:

Prefer a Product – 66.7%

Prefer a Webinar – 33.3%

Now, I should qualify these numbers by saying this is a strictly non-scientific and self-selecting survey. So, they might not hold water in every single list and for single niche.

Plus, a few people said they would prefer one over the other, but would be happy with either, or that they would quite like both.

But, the results are 2:1 in favour of a product, and so the 12 Minute Strategy will in the form of a product.

I want to paraphrase some of the comments, I received, to give you an idea of popular thinking about this:

Pros For A Product

- some people find it hard to clear time in their schedule to attend a webinar, and have less interest in watching a recording.

- a webinar is not suitable for people who have hearing difficulties.

- there are also international subscribers (and, I imagine, some people in more rural areas) who just can't follow webinars as the right telephone infrastructure is either not in place, or the bandwidth costs are just too expensive.

Pros For A Webinar

- people like the live nature and interactivity of a webinar.

- UK based subscribers (like me) like the idea of attending a webinar at times convenient to them.

One question I didn't directly ask, but which was raised in the comments, was whether the product would be a written or video product. I certainly envisioned this being a video product in either case (whether presented live on a webinar, or as prerecorded videos), mainly because the nature of what I intended to show was visual.

But, many of the issues raised in favour of the product solution rather preclude the idea of a video product.

The Compromise

I'm still planning on a product involving video, as this is the only way I see myself being able to provide the right information.

One, often suggested solution, is to provide transcripts. The sales of my products aren't at a stage where this is something I can deliver, unfortunately, but it's something that I hope to strive towards. This is something for marketers who are more established to seriously consider.

A transcript also provides some value for webinar recordings as well, and hopefully answers some objections.

In this case, I'm planning to include a Quick Start Guide, with the highlights of the videos, but with nowhere near the level of detail. I know that's not a perfect solution, but I hope it's of some use.

So, Are Webinars Dead?

Definitely not.

The fact of the matter is that they do appeal to a sector of the audience. It's generally impossible to meet every possible customer with every product, so a bit of a 'balancing act' is necessary. I certainly intend to use webinars in the future where they are an appropriate fit.

And, from a personal point of view, the idea of appealing to the UK market appeals to me. The good thing about this is that, a webinar scheduled in the evening (UK time) is the afternoon (North American), so it's possible to time it well for that market too.

Some marketers like to create a product, then offer a webinar as a bonus, and that's another viable solution to consider.

Five Ways To Fill Your Autoresponder

How often do you e-mail your list?

If you're anything like most marketers, it probably isn't enough.

You need to e-mail your list often enough so that they know who you are, but not so much that they get sick or tired of you.

Depending on your niche, this could be anything from once a day, to once a week, but the ideal best frequency is probably somewhere between the two.

But, what can you send them? Here's five quick-and-easy ways to get you going

Way #1

A link to your most recent blog post.

Way #2

Remind them of one of your accounts: your Twitter, your Facebook, or your blog.

Way #3

Send them a question. It could be related to a blog post or a product you're developing.

Way #4

Send them a free gift. Just compile a simple e-book, or use PLR, brand it, and you have something which can be valued.

Way #5

Send a promotion. It can be one of your offers, or someone else's.

The important thing about all of these is that they can have a call to action. Even with a free gift, you can brand your site in the e-mail and in the report.

Still stuck for ideas? Resend old messages to people who weren't on your list at the time. And resend the same links to people who don't open the first message, or just to ask for more results.

Instant Product System

How often do you find yourself stuck, thinking that you want to release a product, but not knowing what to release it on.

In this blog post I'm going to reveal a very simple method that you use at any time to put out a quick product.

Even better, it will be a low ticket product that people want, and which you can pull together quickly and easily.

The Secret Is To Use Your Personal Experience

You're not messing around trying to research new areas. You're simply taking information and experience that's already in your head and formatting it for a ready market.

People will pay to work more efficiently.

People will pay to copy success.

People will pay so that they don't copy failure.

With that, you have information that anyone who is trying to learn to market will pay for.

The 'System' Product

In this product, you simply reveal the exact process you go through to complete a common task.

This should be something that you have done regularly and that other marketers also do themselves.

You're passing on the little refinements to the process that you've made that make your process faster, more manageable and more effective.

Break this down into a number of simple steps, which are easily replicable.

Then package this as a 'System'.

24

For instance, when I set up a new niche blog there's a certain way I always set it up. The same ways I get the software installed quickly. A set of configuration changes I make. The plugins I use that always make the blog more successful.

I could package up that information quite quickly and soon have a 'System' product ready to sell.

The 'Case Study' Product

In this product, you're telling people about something you've done.

It might have been something that was really successful. It might be something that was only moderately successful, or even a downright failure.

You go through the exact steps you followed, the thought process behind it, and what bits worked. More importantly, you need to talk about what you discovered by doing this, and the changes you would make if you were do this again. This is a 'Case Study'.

Marketers are very rarely willing to share their real world experience. Too much of Internet Marketing is based around theory. By just going out there and showing somethign that you've tried, you're immediately giving much more value than the same regurgitated information that plagues Internet Marketing.

Let me give you an example, which I touched on in my post on the $1 WSO. The theory being tested, that selling a product for $1 is a good list building mechanism. My experience was that it was less effective than the theory led me to believe. What exactly did I try? Why did I try it? How would I make this process more effective next time?

These are all questions I could address in a comprehensive 'Case Study' product.

Produce Your Instant Product

Think about it for a minute. I'm sure there are ideas you've tested which you could document. I'm sure there are marketing tasks you complete regularly that you've got down to a fine art.

Don't sit on this information. Put it into a product, whether it's an e-book, a video product, or even a webinar. Failing that, at least use it for a series of interesting blog posts.

I certainly plan to push up the schedule with my own Instant Products.

The $1 WSO – Does It Work?

Today, I want to share some information with you that I've never seen shared in public before.

It's the result of a recent list building experiment I tried using the $1 WSO method.

For the uninitiated, the Warrior Forum is an Internet Marketing forum. WSO stands for Warrior Special Offer. It's an area of the site in which marketers can pay to advertise their own product.

Background

I recently ran a $1 WSO selling a proven product. A lot of marketers recommend this type of WSO. The stated benefit of the $1 WSO is not financial, but is from capturing proven buyers onto your e-mail list.

In fact, out of every $1, only 66c is transferred to your PayPal account. The rest goes in PayPal fees. So, financial motivation should definitely not be a reason for running one of these WSOs.

It is about delivering to customers. The buyers benefit from a quality product, worth much more than the $1 spent.

The $1 offer was live for 48 hours. During the WSO, the product amassed 716 views, which is a good number for anything in the WSO Forum.

The cost of running the WSO was $40.

Exactly 60 sales were made, for takings (after PayPal fees) of $39.60.

So, this was a breakeven experiment.

(actually, the sales themselves made a very slight profit for reasons which I will go into another time – although the product acquisition costs meant an overall loss. Of course the product is still on sale, just not at the WSO price).

What does all this mean?

It means that the $1 WSO can work and it can, with the right offer, be a low risk proposition for both the buyer and seller (and in internet marketing, spending $40 is a pretty low risk).

The gains however, may be relatively modest, depending on how you value 60 new buyers and subscribers.

In my case, I consider it a success, but not an overwhelming success. But enough of a success to try it again in a few months with another suitable product.

So, if you are considering running a $1 WSO, go ahead. Don't overthink it. You will see results.

Get More Out Of Coaching Programmes

I've been having an interesting back and forth dialogue recently with William Cato, all related to online training and coaching.

That prompted my post today.

I'm sure, like me, you hear a lot about taking advantage of coaching and training programmes (and maybe even how to deliver a good one). But, you hear much less about how to take advantage of the programme once you're a member.

I've come up with three things you really should be doing when you're being coached to get maximum value out of your investment. They're all simple to carry out. You can integrate them directly into the coaching.

And they'll pay off for you in the long run.

Complete The Challenges!

This sounds so simple, but so many people enrol on a course and just don't complete the challenges as they go along.

Think about studying at a school, or at college. You'd expect to get regular homework, which the teacher would grade and give back to you, hopefully accompanied with some ideas about where you could improve.

An online course is just the same. You need to continual 'course correction' to make the best use of the training you've paid for. And, if you don't complete the activities along the way, you just won't get it.

It's not like school. Nobody's going to chase you up if you don't do it. You have to have a personal reason to want to succeed.

Plus, a lot of people just don't think of getting the most out of the training, by being able to ask (and receive answers to) informed questions. I certainly want to be able to get direct help and clarification when I'm on a course. Even better, is to be able to point to something I've tried and which just hasn't succeeded.

That's why completing challenges is so important.

Communicate In The Members' Area

Every good online course has a membership area, where you can talk to the other participants.

Don't be a lurker.

You want to be popping into the members' area regularly to find out what the other people on the course are doing. Look out for their names. These are people who can be your contacts online.

And, online contacts are so important. You need to have them.

What better people than ones who have already proven that they're interested in the same subjects as you, and who are proven to have money (like you, they've invested in training).

So go ahead, help them out if they're stuck and you know the answer. It will assist you in the long run.

Don't Do The Bare Minimum

This is in some ways a combination of the two methods I've already described, but, generally, you'll get out of the course what you put in.

If you do just the bare minimum, you really can't expect to get anything other than the bare minimum back out.

If you do more than the bare minimum, you'll get more out.

Part of this will just be a direct result for you. If you've just found out how to set up a new Wordpress blog, then why stick at one? Set up a second for extra credit.

It won't get you any more marks or a second qualification. What it will get you is an additional income stream from the second blog that you set up.

Likewise, being active in the members' area adds to your name recognition. Take it upon yourself to post useful links, provide mentorship and encouragement to the other participants, even show off what you've done (without being too big headed).

Whatever you can do to enhance your success rate is of value.

You Make Your Own Success!

Too many course takers just don't realise this.

Like with your own marketing efforts, what you get back out will be directly proportional to what you put in.

This is doubly true for being coached.

Be the star student!

Grow Your List With Your Next Blog Post Idea

I wanted to throw out an idea to you today that I've personally used recently to grow my list. It's all based around thinking about content that was destined for your blog, but repurposing it in a different way.

Now, although my example is aimed towards the online marketing niche, as that's where my heart is at right now – there's no reason why these tactics won't work for any niche you might be involved with. Just substitute the traffic sources I recommend for ones in your own niche, and you're away.

Here's the idea, and the challenge for you.

Instead of writing the next post for your blog, develop that into a report that you can give away to build your mailing list.

Choose The Right Post

Almost any detailed post that you'd be willing to place on your blog can be easily made into a free report. I'm assuming, of course, that you write quality posts for your blog. If you think they're of variable quality, just choose one of the best ones. With this method, you can even take a post that you've already published on your blog and update it in the manner I'm going to show you to give you a new product.

You need to start off with a typical catchy blog post.

The kind of posts I think work well are:

- Three Mistakes That You Make When Doing X

- Four Steps To Achieve Y

- Five Things You Must Know About Z

I like to use numbers, as anything you can break down in than manner is easier to write about. You can just treat it as a series of separate chunks, rather than one long document.

Writing The Report

You write the free report in exactly the same way as you would have written the blog post. The main difference is that you go into more detail with each of these chunks. Plus, you add more of an introduction about yourself, and you make sure to include some useful resources at the end of the report (whether these are your own online assets or ones that you're promoting as an affiliate).

As well as adding more detail, you can incorporate more images and examples within the report. One area I like to use in these reports is personal results. You can report these as a 'case study'. Readers like to know how well things actually work.

For a case study to be a success, you don't actually have to have made a fortune with it. Marketers are becoming much wiser to Guru products and they're looking for applicable and workable results from people on the same level as them. That means, people who don't have a huge email list, or massive existing following of rabid buyers. So, your lower level results can be just as appealing in the modern marketplace.

Your free report can be anywhere from 10 pages in length and up. Now, that may sound a lot, but by the time you've counted out title pages, disclaimers and resources, you may only have 5 or 6 pages of contents. At 300 words a page, you're looking at writing the equivalent of 4 articles of 450 words each. That's something which is easily doable in an hour, or two hours if you're a slow writer.

Advertising The Free Report

You can write more, and if you enjoy writing this can be beneficial for the long term. Slap a price tag on the short report (I suggest sticking with the typical price of $7), but offer this for free for a limited period, in exchange for an email optin. This element of scarcity will help you to draw in names for your email list.

Put the report behind a simple squeeze page and you're ready to advertise.

Online Marketing Success – Volume #1: The Best Of The Blog

For Internet Marketing products, I suggest that you advertise in the Warrior Special Offers Forum. I recently wrote a report along these lines, and you can see the results with my product **Insider WSO Tips**. This report, detailing 7 tips I'd observed to have more success in the Warrior Forum, could easily have been a blog post, but just needed a little expansion to make it into a viable list building report.

In my case, I decided to offer the report for free for 48 hours, which got me about 100 downloads. I also covered the cost of advertising on the Warrior Forum through an upsell product.

One mistake I probably made was making this initial offer on a weekend, where traffic is on the Warrior Forum is usually lower. I'd imagine that I'd have done better by offering this initial 48 hour period starting on a weekday.

The important point is that this system is replicable, and providing you're able to write a report, set up a squeeze page, and add a small amount of sales copy to go with it, then you can easily grow an email list. It worked for me.

This short report needn't take you much longer to put together than a decent blog post and will be much more profitable for you in the long run.

Conclusion

There are some powerful ideas in this physical volume if you just take what you've discovered and apply it.

Just the list building techniques alone are well worth following. Use giveaway events to build your list following the simple process I described to you. Then make sure you follow up with your list regularly.

The $1 WSO is another great list building mechanism

Do join coaching and training programmes. They're very valuable if you use them right.

If you are looking to get started, and would like to be coached to avoid making the mistakes I made when I started out, I recommend you check out **WSO Coaching**.

http://wsocoaching.com

Have a great day wherever you are, and be sure to check in to my blog if you want to read more posts.

To Your Success!

Thom Lancaster

Thom Lancaster

Resources

Online Marketing Sale
http://onlinemarketingsale.com

Online Marketing Success Blog
http://thomlancaster.com

Thom Lancaster's Twitter
http://twitter.com/thomlancaster

Earn 1K A Day Insider's Club
http://thomlancaster.com/e1k

All My Instant Commission Products
http://thomlancaster.com/rapbank

Free Report – Insider Tips Revealed
http://thomlancaster.com/topposts

WSO Coaching
http://wsocoaching.com

10 Buck PLR
http://10buckplr.com

12 Minute Articles
http://12minutearticles.com

The Forum Formula
http://forumformula.com

Writing Content For Sale
http://writingcontentforsale.com

Mobile Market Magic
http://mobilemarketmagic.com

International Internet Marketing
http://international-internet-marketing.com

www.ingramcontent.com/pod-product-compliance
Lightning Source LLC
Chambersburg PA
CBHW051250170526
45165CB00004B/1644

* 9 7 8 1 4 5 3 8 6 9 2 0 8 *